D0941900

THE BALLET-LOVER'S COMPANION

Uniform with
THE BALLET-LOVER'S POCKET-BOOK
by the same Author

AMBROSE

Celia Franca &
Paul Gnatt

Les Sylphides

The Ballet-Lover's Companion

A GUIDE TO
PRACTICAL AESTHETICS

BY

Kay Ambrose

Adam and Charles Black
Soho Square London W.1

Dedicated to
CELIA FRANCA

whose inspiration and beauty are equalled
only by her love and understanding
of the art of ballet, and by her patience with
her grateful friend
KAY AMBROSE

ACKNOWLEDGEMENTS

My gratitude and thanks are due to Mme Karsavina, for advice and encouragement ; to Mme Volkova, for permission to watch classes and for special information concerning the training of the arms ; to M. Stanislas Idzikowski, at whose classes many of these sketches were made, and whose patience and knowledge are inexhaustible ; to Mme Rambert, who carries more ballets in her head than could be contained in any book; M. Léonide Massine, for a discussion on music, and Mr. Frederick Ashton for one on choreography; Col. de Basil, and Mr. Antony Tudor for permission to watch and sketch ballets; Miss Kathleen de Vos, for practical assistance, and Mr. Walter Gore, for certain corrections.

Steps were specially demonstrated and posed by Mmes Vera Volkova, Celia Franca, Anne Lascelles and Joyce Graeme ; and by Messrs. Stanislas Idzikowski, Poūl Gnatt, Henry Danton and Erik Brūhn.

General information was extracted from countless dancers, sketches of some of whom the reader may recognise ; to them all, my grateful acknowledgements.

Documentary information of all kinds, as contained in about a score of Mr. Cyril W. Beaumont's books, has been freely employed. Mr. Lionel Bradley gave invaluable assistance in providing elusive names and dates.

FIRST PUBLISHED 1949 REPRINTED 1949 AND 1951
PRINTED IN GREAT BRITAIN BY R. & R. CLARK, LTD., EDINBURGH

CONTENTS

PRELUDE

The vision of beauty is spontaneous, in just the same sense as the inward light of the lover. It is a state of grace that cannot be achieved by deliberate effort, though perhaps we can remove hindrances to its manifestations, for there are many witnesses that the secret of all art is to be found in self-forgetfulness. And we know that this state of grace is not to be found in the pursuit of pleasure ; the hedonists have their reward, but they are in bondage to loveliness, while the artist is free in beauty.

ANANDA COOMARASWAMY, *The Dance of Siva*, Chapter IV.

FOREWORD

1. EXPLANATION AND ACKNOWLEDGEMENT

How many dancers deserve the title of *artist*, and how many people are entitled to say which one is an artist, and which one is not ?

Now, since a ballet-dancer can scarcely be a bore and an artist at the same time, one may safely admit that the public can recognise an artist, in a reasonable setting, almost on sight. There are also a number of people whose sense of values is so highly tuned that they can sense a good artist without being able to give an account of their reasons, just as some sporting people can sense a winning horse. Then there are the people of intelligence, amongst whom one may remark a large percentage of old ladies, who seem to know exactly who is a ballerina and who is merely masquerading under the title ; and a few others.

In between the public and the groups of people of special discernment, uncertainty and prejudice is the order of the day, and in this department one finds most of the student dancers, some of the dancers themselves, and a motley collection of writers and " critics ". Most of the latter, having little time to spend on a conscientious study of art and its trappings, are involuntary members of the " I know what *I* like " brigade. We are not concerned with them, nor they with us, as they are without doubt perfectly happy as they are.

The person to whom this book is addressed is he who is not content with adopting the prejudices of others, nor with the verdict of the casual theatre-goer ; but is one who wants to discover some workable basis upon which he can form and defend his own tastes.

In order to do this, the lover of ballet secures what books he can on the subject of dancing. Before long, he discovers that literature on ballet is sharply divided into certain categories. First, the books devoted to loading laurels on to the popular figures of the dancing world ; second, the books on the technical side of dancing ; and then the ones on the aesthetic side. The biographies and autobiographies are almost the only ones which have perforce to combine the technical side with the aesthetic side of dancing. Perhaps the only book which intentionally combines these inseparable qualities in dancing is Noverre's *Letters on Dancing*, of which more will be said later on.

Thus it can happen that one may study dancing for years, and yet remain completely in the dark with regard to what may be termed the practical ethics of dancing, and as it has been proved a fatal mistake to study dancing and leave the ethics to take care of themselves, this book is addressed to dancers, as well as to their admirers.

The prospect of addressing dancers with reference to any subject relating to dancing would have filled me wth the liveliest embarrassment, were it not that the dancers themselves have encouraged me to do so. They point out that the predecessor to this book, which was addressed to the followers of ballet, was much appreciated by the dancers themselves ; therefore, why should not a book which is mainly concerned with dancers' problems, be of interest to their audiences ?

Thus emboldened, I immediately enlisted their assistance. The results are in this book. Comprehensive acknowledgements are, once more, out of the question ; I have sought information far and wide, and a condensed version of my findings appears in these pages. Sometimes I am indebted to several people for one sketch, and to a dozen more for the notes underneath it. Generally speaking, I have made acknowledgements to these people whose time I have stolen to the greatest extent.

I cannot find words with which to express my gratitude to all those who have so unselfishly given me their help : their enthusiasm, their demonstrations, their suggestions of every kind ; their forbearance, when I asked involved questions demanding simple answers ; their impartiality, in sending me from one to the other for information ; their modesty, which, allied to their love of their art, makes of them a group of people worthy of that respect and love which it is my privilege, and that of countless others, to accord them.

2. *AESTHETICS : THE DANCER'S DEFINITION*

The word *aesthetics*, according to the dictionary, means " the feeling of beauty in objects, the principles of taste and art ". If there was an alternative, a less-abused word which was equally suitable, I should gladly use that instead. Aestheticism is a word which is most used by those that understand it least, consequently, at present it has what may be termed horn-rimmed associations, and also a vague connection with pompousness and *chi-chi*.

Nevertheless, it is this strong feeling for beauty which first causes a child to want to become a ballet-dancer (a desire for physical movement alone usually indicates a career in sport). If genuine, and properly nurtured, that feeling for art will survive, and become the aesthetic quality of the finished dancer. As the years go by, however, and the technique of ballet-dancing becomes increasingly difficult to acquire, that priceless feeling for beauty has to survive a great deal of hard, mechanical training, one might almost say drudgery, and sometimes although the dancer survives, the feeling does not. The involuntary reaction to music, the joy of movement, instead of being developed in the course of the training, becomes submerged in a torrent of militant physical technicalities.

Then we get a dancer who is " cold ". If he knows there is something wrong with his work, he will suffer agonies ; if he is perfectly satisfied with himself, then he remains an uninteresting performer and an irritating personality.

Therefore it is of the greatest importance to attend to the aesthetic side of a dancer's training. It is quite useless to adopt the unproductive attitude, that " either you've *got* the feeling or you just *haven't* ". If that feeling has once been yours, then there is no reason why it should not be encouraged and developed, instead of curbed and extinguished.

Aesthetics, for the ballet-dancer, can and should be included in the course of ordinary training. Their study consists of the perpetual consideration of the practical education of the artist-dancer, and the perpetual adjustment of this education, by the preceptor, to suit each separate pupil.

The aesthetic quality in dancing is the one which distinguishes the artist from the technical acrobat. The difference is that which exists between boredom and stimulation ; in the theatre it is the difference between life and death.

3. *AESTHETICS IN TRAINING : CAUSE AND EFFECT*

Having established the existence of the aesthetic quality in dancing, the next step is to confirm its identity. One way of doing this is to attempt to analyse the precise qualities of certain great artist-dancers but this would get us little further, as it is individuality which distinguishes the artist, and although the most minute consideration of each of the great dancers is an inspiration to us, it is doubtful whether, in this way, we should be able to draw any workable conclusion as to the very essence of this most transient form of art. As it is with this essential artistry that this book is concerned, we will consider the matter, not from the aspect of the great dancers, but from its very source, that is to say, from the point at which a student, who is possessed of all the natural attributes of the great dancer, embarks on his or her serious training as an artist.

His training as an artist should take place concurrently with his technical training—indeed, the two considerations should be synonymous. And here we come to the root of the matter ; it is obvious that when these two factors, art and technique, become separated from one another, ballet ceases to be an art.

The essence of all art is to sound a chord which will find an echo of sympathy in the majority of its spectators or auditors. In ballet, the deep satisfaction we feel after a successful *pas de deux* is due to certain ideals which come to life in all of us ; perhaps we may say " all the world loves lovers ", and thus see it proved. Conversely, after a mechanically performed *pas de deux*, we feel vaguely embarrassed and slightly guilty, as if we had been watching two inexperienced lovers through a keyhole. Anger, jealousy, love, avarice, in their realistic form, are not the concern of the artist-dancer. The passions must be interpreted poignantly, rather than robustly, so that in watching the dancers we feel for them, because they are feeling for us, and expressing that feeling through their movements.

The dancer who can touch us in this manner is one who has mastered subtleties and inflections of movement which, whilst they could never be taught to an insensitive pupil, can be fostered and developed in the normal student during the course of his or her ballet training.

The bulk of the practical material which this book contains deals with the way in which subtleties in training can have a direct bearing on the ultimate subtleties of the dancer's performance.

At first sight, the sketches, diagrams and explanations may seem to have little to do with the development of art, nevertheless, each section contains an example of misinterpretation. In nearly every one of these cases, the misinterpretation consists of failure to perceive the real purpose of the object in question, for example, performing a beautiful pose and showing the wrong view of it to the audience.

This travesty is the result of allowing the aesthetic object of dancing to become separated from the purely mechanical object.

I have had to try to separate certain indivisible elements in ballet in order to consider the construction of the whole, but it is as well to remember that, in practice, it is as difficult as it is in-advisable to separate the aesthetic from the purely mechanical components of dancing.

To dance without feeling is not to dance at all, that is to say, artistically, it is not ballet, however many *pirouettes*, *entrechats*, etc. the dancer may perform. Conversely, one who possesses quantities of emotion, and who cannot master the training of a great academic technique, should shun a career in ballet, and only attempt " greek " dancing or the various " expressionistic " forms of the dance, where the delight of the performer himself is the first consideration. For untrammelled emotion is like an untrained body—unwieldy and unsuitable for the ballet stage.

During the centuries which have seen the development of ballet, preponderance has been given alternately to technical and aesthetic considerations. At the present time the aesthetic quality in dancing is receiving too much of the wrong sort of attention, with writers and spectators so engrossed with their own reactions that the realities of a ballet performance are apt to escape them.

The very basis of our education, in this country, is reserve. That is why so many of our teachers and directors confuse real feeling with the vulgarity of exhibitionism ; and many more, whilst possessing sincere and deep feeling themselves, shrink from analysing their own hearts, in order to help their pupils to develop along the same lines.

4. *TEMPERAMENT AND THE ARTIST-DANCER*

For all general purposes, the term *artist*, used in conjunction with a dancer, has become a purely complementary one, even as the word *artiste*, as it is used to-day, simply implies that someone is pursuing a theatrical career. The term, *temperament*, is widely used to describe the nervous and irritable characteristics attributed to all those associated with the stage.

It is the object of this book to prove that, although the terms " dancer " and " artist " should be synonymous, this is not always the case. A study of the qualities of the genuine artist has been attempted, and this cannot be complete without reference to temperament.

As we have seen, if a dancer is not an artist as well as a trained performer of leaps, postures and steps, then there is little to choose between him and an acrobat (indeed, if the latter is passionately attached to his work, he may well prove the better artist of the two).

The quality which makes an artist of a dancer is one which defies summary. It is closely allied to the passions, and consists of a mixture of sensitivity of the mind, acuteness of the senses and physical control of the body and features.

In the first place, if you possess the soul of an artist, it is useless in dancing unless you are able to express it in a convincing and clearly visible form to an audience.

Secondly, if you have remarkable physical and muscular gifts, superb control and elevation, an audience will remain ignorant of your real powers if you have an apparently cold or placid disposition and are at a loss how to convey any emotion in the form of movement ; that is to say, if you lack the right temperament.

In both these cases, the dancer would earn the title of artist if he balanced his natural gifts by studying those qualities which are not naturally his. There is a third type of dancer, however ; those incapable of any feeling other than that of physical discomfort. Consequently, with no knowledge of the inner meaning of the word, they set about copying its external characteristics, and it is one of the most unpleasant phenomena that can be seen. They confuse weakness with strength, comedy with romance, and tantrums with tragedy ; in short, they mistake temper for temperament.

It is useless to point out that they should renounce the pursuit of art. They cannot understand the term, and by the same token, neither can they appreciate their own shortcomings. They can, however, talk business, and this is the explanation behind so many mediocre ballet companies to-day, and so many saddened and restless artist-dancers.

Genuine temperament, then, is a form of acute mental sensitivity peculiar to the genuine artist. As such people are, more often than not, persons of good taste, they usually have too much consideration to inflict on other people those wild scenes which are popularly, and wrongly, understood to be the main outward signs of genius. Nevertheless, they feel so strongly about certain matters that sometimes their sense of artistic outrage amounts to violent physical pain, and under these circumstances the smallest incident may be the only apparent cause of a storm. This occasional tempest at first frightens the insensitive spectator, then impresses him. He resolves to give an imitation himself when opportunity offers ; and this is mainly how the word " temperament " has become so grossly misunderstood and misused.

It is a bold writer who will dare to place on record that true temperamental qualities cannot be cultivated. But it can be stated categorically that nothing is to be gained by imitating the outward signs of temperament in others. To take an instance : a painter who lives in squalor is not to be congratulated on the condition of his studio, but on his work. Those who think to improve their own work by imitating the squalor are obviously unintelligent, and do much to degrade their art into what should be their own personal disrepute.

The best breeding-ground in which true temperamental qualities can be cultivated is in the liberal use of the brain. Study music, study literature and the arts ; in moderation, study yourself ; bring intelligence to bear on all you do. Thus you will develop your own standards, without which you will be incapable of judging yourself, or anyone else. Instead of harbouring that negative sensation, jealousy, you will learn to profit by the example of great dancers, and even if you don't become a great dancer in your own estimation, yet if you work thus hard and sincerely, you will find that other people's opinion of your progress will grow in proportion to your own self-respect.

5. *THE LETTERS OF JEAN GEORGES NOVERRE*

It would be idle to attempt to write any survey of the practical aesthetics of ballet without continual recourse to the *Letters on Dancing and Ballets* of Jean Georges Noverre (1727–1810). This great man has been called by Garrick " the Shakespeare of the dance ", and likened to Prometheus by Voltaire, who affirms that Noverre should " first make men, and then make them move ".

I have heard disillusioned artists and dancers say that " it is so depressing to read that Noverre's problems in the eighteenth century were just the same as ours to-day ". This attitude is one which shows that the real value of the *Letters* has not been perceived, and it is to be hoped that the majority of readers will take advantage of the comforting reflection that Noverre had not only found the cause of, and the practical solution to those very problems, but he left us an account of how he was able to effect his revolution, which he says, in one of his prefaces to his published *Letters*, " is as great as the musical revolution effected by Glück ".

Noverre was one of those rare people whose character effectually combined common sense with good taste and a flaming and passionate love of his art, which he was sufficiently level-headed to control. On the stage, he presented the superb results of this well-balanced mixture of taste, learning and originality to the public of his day. The present-day reader can study his analyses of his own works in this remarkable book.

There are few people who can read Shakespeare without finding in his work continual observations and allusions which bear directly upon present-day events and circumstances. In the same way, the lover of ballet and art will find that his is indeed a strange problem if Noverre has not dealt with it and suggested its cause and solution. The *Letters* encompass the dancer, his physique, training and even his diet ; the construction of ballets from every point of view ; quarrels, jealousies and conceits. Noverre pursues his creed, for the most part, with measured calm, but flashes of wit and temper occasionally combine to make one admire the man for his courage. He made terrible enemies, but his unselfish love for his art overrode social considerations at a gallop, even when he knew he was risking his own financial position and immediate career.

The *Letters* have been ably and subtly translated, printed and published by Mr. Cyril W. Beaumont, to whom both dancers and their admirers are already so deeply indebted for his own conscientious and informative books. Noverre should be the delight of the ballet-lover and of any connoisseur ; a constant inspiration to the dancer ; and a veritable bible to the choreographer. He is much quoted in this book.

6. *ON MAÎTRES DE BALLET*

The popular practice of pigeon-holing sections of society, which stipulates that all genuine professors are vague, all real artists dirty, and so forth, would have us believe that all *bona-fide* teachers of dancing should possess and display a vicious temper. Instances of malevolence are cited, not with the purpose of shocking the hearer, but rather to impress him with the great gifts of the teacher.

Thus it becomes necessary to insist that the behaviour of a teacher is only incidental to the quality of his teaching. (The often-repeated story of the famous conductor, who seized the first fiddle's violin and broke it to show his disapproval of the orchestra's performance, has done little to improve that conductor's musical reputation, which was presumably built up on his performance as a conductor, and not on personal attacks on his musicians, as the sensation-mongers would like us to credit.)

Because one teacher is vociferous and condemnatory and has good pupils, it does not follow that one who is gentle and courteous does not also obtain excellent results. A young pupil may learn more easily from one than from the other, but this is due to the obvious difference between the nervous and the lazy pupil.

The mature pupil should be able to learn something from every established teacher.

But I have known a woman whose daughter had learned hitherto from a somewhat loquacious teacher, to take her away from the class of a celebrated continental *maître de ballet*. " He never made any corrections, and hardly spoke at all ", she complained.

If dancers were made by speaking, what a wealth of virtuosos there would be !

(*N.B.*—In English, the term *maître de ballet* means a teacher of dancing. Used in a French context, it also means a choreographer.)

7. *ON THE DANCER AS AN INDIVIDUAL*

It has been very difficult to divide this book into separate sections. Each problem seemed to spring from the same cause and, when logically unravelled, to have basically the same solution.

For example : let us compare the case of the dancer who is gifted technically and physically, but who remains unnoticed on the stage, an unsatisfactory performer, and the dancer who gives a marvellous performance, but who has an unreliable technique and certain physical disadvantages. At first sight, one might suppose that their problems have quite different causes. On consideration, however, one realises that they have probably received exactly the same sort of training, which suited neither, and that their teachers were too inflexible to develop their separate talents and help them, at the same time, to remedy their inherent disadvantages. Therefore, these two dancers, so widely different, are suffering from precisely the same malady. It is only superficially that they should be treated differently from one another ; basically, that very difference should spring from one source, which is the diagnosis and development of the individual.

Clearly, if I were to pursue this line of reasoning, this book would run into several volumes, whilst the point itself would become obscured. Therefore, in this case and throughout these pages, I have confined myself to the introduction of carefully chosen lines of thought which I sincerely believe will be profitable to the reader, if he develops them himself.

8. *GENERAL NOTES ON TEACHERS AND PUPILS*

J. G. Noverre accused the dancers of his day of indolence and sloth. One of the reasons he named to prove their laziness was their refusal to pay any attention to a certain treatise on dancing by a Monsieur de Cahusac. This treatise dealt with dancing in its aesthetic sense as well as in general ; and (as the reader will have discovered), since even the simplest discussion of aesthetics in dancing means much earnest thought, the dancers were not disposed to take the trouble to study this volume. They poured scorn on, and poked fun at, de Cahusac and his beliefs ; and Noverre, confronted by dancers who had learned dancing " less to escape a more tranquil profession than to enjoy the pleasures they think to encounter . . ." and finding it difficult to carry out his choreographic intentions with such material, set about making their ears tingle with conspicuous success.

To-day, in the world of dancing the same sort of situation exists. It has become a habit amongst dancers to complain of bad teachers, and vice versa ; but most of the persons concerned have shown themselves to be more than reluctant to practise any exacting method of dancing, which requires the students to attempt difficult but unsensational feats, rather than to display those movements which they can already master. Even as in Noverre's day, they readily attend classes which afford them an opportunity to show their natural elegance and talents, but they do not seem prepared to try to master what cannot be easily performed, in the way of *adages* and exercises.

Anyone who speaks with favour of the system of the late Maestro Enrico Cecchetti will find himself in the predicament of some hard-working student or scholar, who is considered a traitor by his lazier fellows because he works hard and conscientiously, and causes the professor to make critical comparisons.

To get the best out of Cecchetti, this master must be thoroughly understood. Any scientific experiment is apt to go astray if the equipment is mishandled by the experimenter. Cecchetti's system of exercises and *enchaînements* are not designed only for elegance in the classroom, but for the acquisition of strength and that complete control without which a dancer's stage performance will always be, at best, erratic.

It is clear that a dancer should always do his best on the stage, but it is a mistake to think that he should only make supreme physical efforts when before the public. The classroom is the place in which physical effort, for its own sake, should be practised. On the stage, the dancer should use his utmost skill and artistry, but he should only exert those technical powers which are already his ; he should never attempt any physical experiments in public, when he is uncertain of the result.

Therefore, the dancer who has a great technical control has a great advantage over the dancer who has brilliant technical capabilities, but who lacks control ; indeed on the ballet stage, the *virtuoso* often seems to be surpassed in technique by the purely skilful dancer. Furthermore, when a dancer who has traded on his technical gifts, and has not troubled himself with the science of dancing in its musical and artistic aspects, reaches maturity, he immediately starts to lose all his powers, as he has absolutely nothing with which to replace the ardour and unconscious physical *attaque* of youth. Whereas the " scientific " dancer, who has learned to weave spells as well as to perform physical wonders, who does everything consciously, can grow greater and greater, as Léonide Massine has shown us.

Properly interpreted, the Cecchetti method teaches just that control. With such an ally as technical and physical mastery on his side, the dancer has far greater freedom to experiment with the expressive and artistic side of theatrical art, and gains the greatest profit from the lessons and examples of other great teachers and dancers.

There are many great teachers of dancing now living, and it would be ridiculous, and contrary to my intention, to try to stipulate that they should all teach in the Cecchetti style. Individuality in teachers is as important as individuality in dancers : the fame of both dancer and teacher should live on through the work of his pupils. Cecchetti's pupils included the divine Karsavina, and he was the *maître de ballet* of the glittering array of prodigious artists which took Paris and the world by storm during the reign of the artistic mammoth, Diaghileff. When Cecchetti died, however, his work did not die with him, for he had established certain rules, methods and routines for every day of the week, which have survived his death ; since when he has, as it were, posthumously trained many pupils with outstanding success.

That the method of Enrico Cecchetti was not only entrusted to the erratic memory of man, is due to the conscientious work of the celebrated dancer and teacher, Mr. Cyril Beaumont, and M. Stanislas Idzikowski, who placed the dancing world even deeper in their debt by compiling a book during the lifetime of Cecchetti, in which his method is excellently propounded.

It would be entirely false if I were to give the impression that dancers should only pay attention to teachers of the Cecchetti method. It cannot be made too clear that a bad *maître de ballet* can harm his pupils through any system he cares to affect, whereas a good teacher can elevate his pupils through his own example, personality and system. When Jules Perrot presented Carlotta Grisi to a delighted public in the eighteen-thirties, as his pupil and partner, there is no doubt that the system he employed to train this legendary dancer was none other than his own.

In conclusion, there seems to be an unspoken belief amongst ballet-pupils that it is their teachers who must do all the hard work. That is to say, it is assumed that if the pupil attends regular classes of a given number of hours a day he will therefore improve, and that if he does not it is the teacher's fault.

But it must be stressed that even if a dancer works daily until he is sweating profusely and tired out, if he is habitually lazy with his mind, he will not improve, and the teacher cannot be blamed.

9. *PREAMBLE FOR THE READER*

To make unqualified statements is a risky business, since it paves the way for contradiction and offence. But if I give a full explanation of every point I wish to make, in order to prevent possible misunderstanding, this book will assume enormous proportions. Therefore, as I cannot always give even two sides of a many-sided question, I have arranged the following chapters so that they substantiate and elucidate one another.

It is the exception which often proves the rule, and this must be admitted, but it should remain an admission and not become a policy. Any technique evolved from exceptions alone would be a most unreliable affair. Whereas the performance of a certain dancer may justify any peculiarities of training, in this book we are concerned only with those rules which can be applied generally and with safety.

Where the demonstrations of particular dances and steps are concerned, these are included as an illustrative example of the point in question, and are not submitted as a model which must be copied in every detail. The intelligent reader will easily appreciate that the purpose of such examples is more analytical than dictatorial.

In the course of these analyses, the attempt has been made to present the material so that it will be of interest to the dancer, and at the same time will not be too technical to amuse and interest the casual reader and those lovers of dancing who want to develop their own standards but who " simply don't know where to begin ".

10. *OVERTURE TO CHAPTER I*

The technical steps displayed in *The Ballet-Lover's Pocket-Book* are danced by figures which, although some of them are immature, are all well-proportioned. Unfortunately, in real life, few people are perfectly made, and dancers are no exception to this rule.

In some cases the fault lies with Nature, and can be cured by a careful and clever teacher; in others the faults are due to bad training itself, which amounts to a number of bad habits, the effects of which are notoriously hard to eradicate.

Bowed-legs and knock-knees can, in many cases, be cured, but when the malformation takes the form of curved thigh-bones, for example, this can only be cured in earliest infancy, if then.

The reader may want to know : what is the link between such dry physical facts and the study of the aesthetic side of dancing ? A link there is, and a most significant one. Any dancer who has had to combat an obstinate physical disadvantage gains much strength of character, which another, a perfectly formed and gifted dancer, may easily lack. But the dancer with natural facility—unless Nature has also gifted her with unusual modesty, sense and determination—may present that not unusual phenomenon : the raving beauty who is artistically dumb.

Therefore, those dancers who are dispirited by some physical disadvantage should take heart. If ill-health could prevent a dancer from dancing, we are told that the theatrical world would have lost Anna Pavlova ; if the struggle with technique could not be won by courage, perseverance and artistry, Olga Preobrajenskaya's brilliance would never have been seen, and the ballet would have been deprived of her marvellously trained pupils, of whom familiar examples are Baronova, Riabouchinska and Toumanova.

It is true that many artists of all kinds are basically lazy, and that lacking some incentive, they may not reveal their real powers. It is equally true that artists who have suffered privation have a wider field of inspiration, and a better conception of human values than their luckier fellows.

It is also true that privation has, in the past, prevented innumerable artists from doing creative work, and thus deprived us of much of that which we can ill afford to lose.

All great artists provide material for their successors to study. It is those who have made deductions and discoveries, and thus established certain rules, who have left us clear lessons which may be learned to-day ; it is those whose genius flamed, unexplained and unquenchable, who provide us with the inspiration and the temerity to attempt the impossible.

NOTES ON THE FOLLOWING CHAPTERS

i. *Technical terms*

Throughout the following chapters I have done my best to avoid any save the simplest technical terms, and most of these are clearly illustrated. There is no space here to include an illustrated glossary of steps, but the reader can be referred to *The Ballet-Lover's Pocket-Book* which, uniform with this volume, contains illustrations and descriptions of all steps used but not described in these pages.

ii. " *Les Sylphides* "

Presented in 1909, and still in the repertoire of any leading company, extracts from this ballet have been chosen to prove many points in this book : (*a*) because most ballet-lovers have seen it and are likely to do so again, and (*b*) because Fokine's sensitive choreography, constructed with the simplicity of the great master, has suffered much clumsy handling in recent years. It is to be hoped that the ballet-lover will pause in future before he accuses of dullness what should be a moving and beautiful work.

iii. *The " awkward " dancers*

In some cases, it may seem that the worst aspect of a dancer has been chosen in preference to the best. Such examples are not chosen from any uncharitable motive, but to establish a certain point with force and clarity.

iv. *The angles of the figures*

To avoid unnecessary foreshortening of the limbs, I have drawn the figure standing at an angle of 45 degrees to the spectator, whenever this does not interfere with the continuity of a step. (E.g. *à la 4e*, p. 38.)

v. *To " read " the technical sketches*

Turn this book upside down and place it on the ground in front of you, when the right and left sides of the sketched figure will correspond with your own.

vi. *The " thumb-reference "*

The " thumb-reference " at the head of each right-hand page is designed to help the reader, when he is referred from one chapter to another.

CHAPTER I

ON BASIC TRAINING

1. DEPORTMENT

The girl on the left has had a bad training. She has always done her best, when at the *barre*, to comply with her instructions, and these have been something like this: " Pull your shoulders back, look up, give yourself a long neck, make yourself as tall as you can, try to make your shoulder-blades meet, tuck your tail in and turn your feet out ".

Some results of this basic training are as follows: an apparently short neck; a flat chest, from undue stretching of the pectoral muscles; weak ribs, and consequently, bad breathing; a protuberant diaphragm, which accentuates an arched or " dancer's " back; this, in turn, draws attention to an over-developed and tilted posterior. The thighs and legs tend to thicken, and are in fact crooked. The dismal list is concluded by weak and rolling feet, because the dancer is trying to turn them out independently, and this is not possible when the hips and knees are turned in. She is strained in appearance, and is leaning heavily on the *barre*. Her career will be short, as she will soon be " muscle-bound". Her movements are hampered and restricted by the unnecessary bulkiness occasioned by her training, and she easily becomes exhausted.

The girl on the right looks far more at ease. She is neither rigid, nor slack, because her shoulders are neither round nor over-drilled. The stomach and posterior are both drawn in, and when the lower pelvis is also advanced, it is unnecessary to consider " tucking the tail in " as a separate objective. Her head is level on her neck and shoulders, and this is the result of trying " to push out the back of her neck " rather than curving it by raising her chin. She is firmly placed, because she has not concentrated solely on turning out her feet, but also her hips and knees ; the feet then turn out by themselves, and it is only necessary to make sure that the ankles do not roll, and that the feet grip the floor almost as if the toes were fingers and perfectly flat on the ground. Her hand is lightly placed on the *barre*. It will be noticed that her weight is evenly distributed between her two feet, whereas the centre of gravity of the girl on the left is well forward, most of her weight being taken on her front foot, and on her hand on the *barre*. Although the girl on the right looks more restful than her companion, she works just as hard. She knows that one of the arts of ballet is to conceal all effort.

In dancing, over-developed muscles are more a sign of weakness than of strength. The girl on this page has control of all her movements, and has therefore an unsuspected store of endurance.

2. ON PHYSICAL ASPECTS

A. *The close-legged dancer (jarreté formation of the legs)*

Nearly every dancer conforms to one of two distinct physical categories : (i) the *close-legged* dancer (featuring the *jarreté* formation of the legs), or (ii) the *bow-legged* dancer (the *arqué* formation). Although both these groups may be described as physically defective, it will be seen that the most important matter is to decide to which group a certain dancer belongs, and to make sure that his training does not accentuate his particular defect, but lessens it, and helps him to overcome all the physical obstacles which would prevent him from enjoying that precision, freedom of movement and *abandon* which is ever the delight of the successful dancer, and of his audience.

Clearly, it is not only inadvisable, but distinctly dangerous, to give exactly the same exercises to dancers who have totally dissimilar physiques. Noverre says, " *Is it not essential to lead them* (the dancers) *to the same end but by different roads ?* " This maxim does not apply solely to bow-legged or close-legged dancers, but to the multiple irregularities of physique, bad habits and involuntary failings with which Nature afflicts every human being, and against which dancers and their teachers must wage an unceasing battle. The dancer and his teacher must decide, between them, upon special exercises and deportment to meet each case. The two examples of leg-formation dealt with in this chapter show the barest essentials of an extremely complicated subject.

The *close-legged dancer*, as the name implies, is one whose thighs and knees are pressed closely together, whilst the ankles are a considerable distance apart. The hips are usually narrow, and the insteps high and beautiful, but often weak. The girls stand on their *pointes* very easily, but need very strongly blocked shoes with very stiff soles.

This type of dancer is usually extremely loose-limbed and supple ; and it is painful to see him continually doing exercises which will make him still more supple, which in this case, means still weaker. He seizes every excuse to perform quantities of *grands battements*, the " splits ", etc. He can throw his legs very high, and this appearance of height is increased by the fact that his knees bend, as it were, the wrong way. Instead of working to strengthen and control his movements, he allows the ill-considered envy of his companions to induce him to exploit his looseness, until his legs look like sticks of damp macaroni, and he becomes unable to regulate his movements to conform to the demands of musical *tempe*.

Instead of this condition of repose and self-satisfaction, the close-legged dancer should study unceasingly the best methods of making his legs appear as straight as possible. To this end, he must turn out his thighs and perform great numbers of *ronds de jambe*, strongly and with vigour, which will help to straighten and strengthen his knees; in addition, he must practise *échappés à la seconde*, and, using the mirror to judge himself, he must relax his knee-joints sufficiently so that his legs appear straight, when in reality they are not so. When he practises *entrechats*, beats, etc., he may again relax his knees slightly, and thus avoid the unpleasant spectacle presented by the thighs and knees, when they seem to roll one upon the other.

If he works hard and unceasingly upon these lines, it will be hard to tell that he suffers from any physical defect; in fact, this training may even effect a genuine cure, and he will delight the spectator with that grace and flowing nobility of movement which is his heritage.

A. The close-legged dancer's natural stance (1st position).

B. The same (on *pointes*, 2nd position).

C. The knees, when slightly relaxed, appear to be straight, avoiding the "mean" appearance of sketch B.

D. An *entrechat* with the knees fully stretched: the heels hardly meet, the knees overlap.

E. An improved position for an *entrechat* with the knees relaxed.

F. Close-legged dancers should beware of positions such as this *grande battement*.

G. The beautiful foot, typical of the close-legged dancer.

H. Carefully trained dancers seldom reveal any imperfections to the spectator. Close-legged dancers excel in *adagio*.

B. *The bow-legged dancer (arqué formation of the legs)*

Those who belong to the *bow-legged* group of dancers are seldom tempted to take life easily. At the outset of their careers, they are usually envious of the close-legged dancer's suppleness and easy grace, of their elegant feet, and general appearance ; this is bad for both groups, as it encourages the close-legged dancer to believe in his own perfections and causes the bow-legged one to bemoan those physical characteristics which can so easily become advantages, if intelligently trained and used.

The bow-legged dancer is usually strongly built, often wide across the hips, vigorous, and in all ways opposite to the other group. His chief occupation should be to try to bring together those parts of his legs which are too greatly separated, principally his knees ; to bring this about, he also must turn out his thighs as much as possible. He is usually " stiff ", by reason of his natural strength, and constantly must practise *grands battements*, and all exercises which will loosen his joints. He must stretch his knees as much as possible on all occasions when the legs should be straight. This task, of making his legs appear quite straight, is further complicated by long, flat feet, which occasion much sorrow and despair to the owner—especially in the case of a girl, who may have difficulty in rising and remaining on her *pointes*. (If such a girl is reading these pages, she should turn to the chapter headed " Practical Notes ", where she will find much to help her with this problem.)

The advantages of the bow-legged dancer are many and heartening. Those long, flat, strong feet enable him to jump great heights, and to land as lightly as a feather. (As one *maître de ballet* philosophically pointed out, " If you can jump, then you usually have a big behind, but there is no need to let it stick out ! ") His *entrechats* and beats are brilliant, because the " light " between his legs accentuates the movements of the feet when *en l'air*, which effect the close-legged dancer has to try to cultivate, by relaxing his knees.

He has that elastic resilience in steps of elevation which is called *ballon*, and which is one of the most sought-after qualities in dancing. The combination of this soft quality in leaping, and the sharp brilliance of his beats, make him an inspiring performer in *temps d'allégro*. To offset this facility, he should practise the slow and precise movements in *adagio* with particular care.

The great dancer, Nijinsky, possessed such astonishing powers of elevation that his leaps have now become a legend. That he also had remarkably developed thighs and the most unusual feet are accessories after the fact ; but those physical peculiarities might have modified his fame as a performer, were it not that his artistry and religious application to his work rendered his physical peculiarities unnoticeable on the stage, though remarkable in the photographs of him which we study to-day.

A. The bow-legged dancer's natural stance (turned in).

B. The improvement when turned out (1st position).

C. His knees tend to look as though they are relaxed when they are stretched.

D1 & D2. The reason for his brilliant *entrechats*. Note the "light" between his legs.

E. A typical foot.

F. Bow-legged dancers excel in *temps d'allégro* and in elevation.

CHAPTER II

ON THE USE OF THE ARMS

1. *INTRODUCTION*

In the days when the *danseuse*'s skirts touched the ground, it was generally assumed that ladies possessed but one leg apiece, and whether that leg was straight or otherwise was of little account. In consequence, their arms came in for the greatest part of their attention ; in fact, in his *Letters*, Noverre cites " voluptuous arms " as one of the " inevitable rocks upon which criticism founders ". To-day, it is to be doubted whether the average standard of our dancer's arm-movements would dazzle the critic sufficiently to blind him to any other shortcomings.

As a rule, a dancer's legs take up by far the largest proportion of his attention ; exercises for the arms are performed simply on the assumption that the result will benefit the arms, *quod erat demonstrandum*. It follows, therefore, that a dancer's arm movements are more haphazard than otherwise, a state of affairs much deplored by Carlo Blasis, who affirmed in 1830, that the dancer who neglected to study his arms had failed to realise that the arms form a frame, which sets off the movements of the body and legs, and that ill-considered arms mar the dancer's performance, in the same way that the value of a picture which is unsuitably framed, or not framed at all, is " unquestionably destroyed ".

Directly the fair sex have been allowed to display their legs, their arm-movements have suffered. This is proved by the present-day performances of period-plays and films, in which the leading ladies look so ill at ease, whilst the more mature actresses, playing the rôles of older women, look perfectly at home. You cannot wear, for example, an Edwardian dress and expect to look like an Edwardian lady, if you cannot make pleasing lines with your shoulders and arms.

Perhaps, in the days of Taglioni and Gardel, the dancers were taught to use their arms as part of their social education, and could thus afford to concentrate on their feet and legs without the ungainly results to be seen to-day.

Our contemporary lack of beautiful and compelling arms is partly due to the dancer's preoccupation with his legs, and partly to his tendency to confine his energies to the exploitation of his natural gifts. If he can jump, if he has a " marvellous *arabesque* ", he continues to try to make himself conspicuous by these means alone, never pausing to consider that the dancer who is also an artist will even relinquish a part of his especial gifts in order to improve his general standard.

2. *PRACTICAL NOTES*

The possessors of abnormally long, or abnormally short arms, should bear in mind that the less time they spend with their arms fully extended, the better. This is not to say that they must avoid all postures which include the extended positions of the arms, for without them dancing could not take place. It means, quite simply, that dancers who have arms which are out of proportion to their bodies should make those movements which precede and follow the extension of their arms as graceful and studied as possible.

To illustrate this point : note that the performer of an *arabesque* should reserve his supreme effort for the moment which occurs just before he relaxes his pose, in which he stretches the line from toe to finger-tip so that it is as long and graceful as can be ;—if he were to adopt this excessively stretched position with undue haste, its principal value would be lost, for the spectator will not have had time to watch the position " grow ", which is the principal pleasure of dancing. The moral to be drawn is that *the beauty and harmony of movement itself will legitimately distract an audience from the study of physical proportions.* Thus the spectator can be encouraged to say " that dancer moves beautifully ", rather than " that dancer standing stock-still has short arms ".

The possessors of normally proportioned arms can make them appear both lovely and eloquent, if they hold them with the wrists and forearms softly aligned, the hands suitably and simply controlled, and the elbows rounded and supported. Those with short arms should take care to hold their hands to give the greatest possible appearance of length, but must be watchful lest the hands become stiff and ungraceful in movement. Those with long arms should curve their wrists and elbows, whilst remaining on their guard against unbecoming angles ; they must control their hands which, as they are usually long and elegant, are inclined to " flap ", and to appear disagreeably affected.

All dancers desirous of improving their arms must regard the mirror with the utmost caution. For instance, a dancer may be convinced that he or she has solved the problem of long arms by undue bending of the elbows and wrists. As the height of the shoulders and arms is near the eye-level, the mirror will make this experiment appear successful. But the view from an altered eye-level, from the stalls or circle, may well be disastrous for the dancer (see p. 30.)

In conclusion, any dancer who makes a serious study of the arms will be amply rewarded by a far more authoritative bearing, and an immense improvement in the apparent height of elevation, etc., but he or she must be prepared to take infinite pains.

Long and short arms

The girls in the sketches below may have had short arms or
long arms—who can tell, what does it matter? If there were
any shortcomings, they remain a secret from us, as from their
lithographers. To dispel the idea that any untrained arms can
look like those of Mlles Grahn and Grisi the reader is invited to
try to imitate these two positions.

On the right : " Imagine you are trying to hug an enormous
hoop." Figs 1, 2 and 3 show a bird's-eye view of this experiment.
1 and 2 are incorrect ; 3 is successful : 3A the correct angle for
the hoop, seen in elevation.

4. A normal arm, extended, but *not* in a ballet-position.
5. A " double-jointed " arm, extended as above.
6. A misinterpretation of a supported elbow, which would lead
    to hard, muscular arms and movements.
7 and 8. Whatever the position of the hands, the elbows should
    remain rounded and supported, whether the hand is palm
    downwards (7), or as in the 2nd position of the arms (8).
    Compare the sketch of Camargo on p. 53 with fig. 8.
9. These two sketches show the arms of the dancer who aims at
    fragility, but only achieves a painfully brittle appearance.
10. The same type of gesture performed more softly, and with
    the elbows supported.
11. *The dancer with long arms.* (A) This girl has decided that
    long arms are an asset, and is making no attempt to control
    them. (B) An attempt to make the arms appear shorter by
    hunching the shoulders and bending the wrists and elbows.
    (C) This girl has attended to her movements and to her whole

Lucile Grahn
in "Eoline, ou la Dryade."

Carlotta Grisi
in "La Péri"

(Circa 1840. From contemporary
lithographs.)

appearance. Her arms have been trained so that their length is unnoticeable, and their apparent shape greatly improved.

12. *The dancer with short arms.* (A) This dancer is determined to do a correct 5th position *en haut*, without even considering her general appearance. (B) This one's idea is to use every inch of her arms, hands and fingers, on all occasions ; thus she draws attention to the shortness of her arms, by continual repetition. (C) This one knows that her arms should not be rounded as in fig. A, nor extended as in B ; but her carefully trained elbows and hands, her poise, and her joy in movement, distract the spectator from studying her proportions.

MIRRORS

1

2 ← DANCER'S VIEW OF HER ARMS

3

VIEW FROM CIRCLE ETC.

VIEW FROM STALLS ETC.

Arms and the mirror

The reflection in mirror No. 2 shows a beginner regarding her arms ; she sees that they look quite smoothly disposed in a good second position. Nevertheless, the reflections in mirrors 1 and 3, which show the dancer respectively from above and below, prove that her elbows and wrists are " broken " ; all her movements will look mean and cramped, and on the stage she will have no authority, and certainly no grace.

The sketches below show one of the countless aspects of the use of the arms in movement. The man in sketch A let his head and shoulders take care of themselves ; the effect of his leap is restricted to the actual distance he can cover. The man in sketch B has studied the placing of his head, shoulders and arms, and his leap will only seem to end when he pleases to relax his pose, the movement being carried on by the direction of his arms, etc. (indicated by arrows) even after he has landed.

A

B

GROUND LEVEL

PREPARATION:
COUNT: (AND 1 ...... 2) EXERCISE: AND ...... 1 ...... AND ...... 2 ...... AND ...... 3 ...... AND ...... 4 ...... ETC:

EXERCISE: COUNT AND ...... 1 ...... AND ...... 2 ...... AND ...... 3 ...... AND ...... 4 ...... ETC:

PREPARATION:
COUNT: AND 1 2

RONDS DE JAMBE À TERRE
with opposed circling of the arms

A. The girl is doing ronds de jambe en dehors (outwards), whilst her arms do "ronds de bras" en dedans (inwards). B shows the exercise reversed. The arm-movements are soft, absolutely continuous and free from jerks : the leg-movements are sharply accentuated each time the foot passes through the first position.

CHAPTER III

ON PRACTICAL SCIENCE

1. *EXPLANATION*

The practical science of dancing is a subject which needs to be approached with extreme caution. Most of us associate the word *science* with the driest of hard facts, but this association is probably due to an uninspired science-master in our early youth. There is a science pertaining to every art—the science of diagnosing those elements which can be codified and passed on to others. If the resulting lesson is found dull, the fault is not in the art in question, but in the unsuitability of either the teacher or the pupil.

In dancing, in addition to the purely physical and mechanical side (which is examined briefly in Chapter I), there is a whole science which covers the practicability of imparting to an audience the emotions which we all experience, but which can only be articulated by the art of movement. It is at this point that dancing becomes an art, for without the means of displaying these emotions the dancer performs only for his own benefit; therefore, if he is the victim of certain technical limitations and has not the skill with which to convey all the human passions to the spectator, the deepest of his feelings will remain unrevealed and his work will be lifeless and uninteresting.

To-day, there is a marked tendency to confuse the purely mechanical aspect of dancing with the more intelligent, scientific aspect. Whilst the mechanics of dancing may be said to concern the actual mastery of one's body, this cannot be fully achieved without scientific study, which concerns the full use of that mastery, i.e. its suitable display and control.

If you confine yourself exclusively to the study of the mechanical side of dancing, you are likely to lose all sense of logic. Your legs may become marvellously " turned out ", but it is probable that you will never realise the purpose of this convention, whereas a fencer or a boxer would tell you that turned-out feet makes it possible to take a quick step in any direction, and to maintain the balance at the same time. If you develop a great elevation and also thick ankles, how are you going to discover, that unless you drop your heels to the ground at the conclusion of each leap, your ankles will get thicker and thicker ?

In the remainder of this chapter, I have tried to indicate the general application of science to movement by a very few practical examples.

2. *NOTES ON BALANCE :* (i) In *adage*

Sketch A, with the leg raised *à la 4ᵉ en avant*, lean forward very slightly. If you try too hard to " tuck your tail in ", you will achieve position B. C, *à la 2ᵉ* : be careful to retract the hip of the working leg, or else—see D. E, *à la 4ᵉ derrière* : here your back is most important. Don't attempt to lift your leg higher than is possible with the back strongly supported, or—see F. *Hint for maintaining the balance in these positions in* adage : the dotted lines represent pieces of string, imagined by the dancer, holding his knee to his waist.

Good equilibrium depends largely on a properly supported back. G, improperly held arms in this 5th position cause an undue arching of the back. H, an improved position. I, rising on *pointes* throws the girl's weight forward ; to counteract this, she leans backwards, causing a deportment which is ugly and harmful to the physique. J, the same girl, having applied the rules for deportment on p. 21.

3

NOTES ON BALANCE : (ii) In *doubles-tours*

A number of students find great difficulty in performing double-turns in the air; and losing the balance at the conclusion of the step is the most common evidence of this failure. A, if you hold your arms as high as this, you will probably overbalance backwards when you land. B, if you try to counteract this by holding the arms a little lower and leaning forward, you are likely to fall on your face. C, the safest method is to hold the arms *à demi.*

THE USE OF THE HEAD IN TURNING

In some forms of turning, the head can remain facing the dancer's front, as in the double-turns shown on the left; or it can move so that the face always seems to be presented to the audience, by a rapid movement of the head from shoulder to shoulder, as shown in fig. 1, above. Here, the dancer (who is perhaps performing a series of diagonal turns), chooses a spot to look at, preferably at the back of the stalls; this spot is represented above by the mark on the placard. 2, the head can lead a turn, as it does in this *tour en renversé en dedans*. 3, *fouettés*. Sketch C is a view of a *fouetté* accorded to the audience by many dancers who perform this step perfectly. A possible reason is advanced by the accompanying diagram, A-B, and a possible solution on the one below, D-E. F shows the correct view of a *fouetté*.

3. NOTES ON ELEVATION

Nos. 1, 2 and 3 above show a *sissone en arrière*, performed with virility and enthusiasm. The deep *plié* (1) throws the dancer far into the air. Nos. 4, 5 and 6 show a version of the same *sissone* performed with a half-hearted *plié*. 8, when performing steps of elevation such as *entrechats*, remember that a plane is helped by its wings, and hold the arms slightly away from the body. *On right*: adjustment of BALANCE IN ACTION. Balance in dancing is not simply a matter of avoiding a fall: in ballet, equilibrium should be used to its fullest extent. In sketches A, 1-7, the girl is performing a *développé à la 4ᵉ devant* (1-4), then a *posé* (5-6) into an *attitude devant* (7). The pleasing *abandon* of fig. 7 is due to the sweeping movement of the *posé* (4-6). Sketches B, 4-7 correspond with the similarly numbered sketches of A above, and show the way in which a final attitude is prejudiced by a "mean" *posé* (B, 4-5). C, 1 shows an arabesque after an inadequate *posé*; C, 2, after a good big step forward.

A

1

2

3

4

5

6

7

(Compare with similarly numbered
sketches above.)

B

4

5

6

7

C

2

1

CHAPTER IV

ON PHYSICAL AND STAGE PERSPECTIVES

1. *EXPLANATION*

It is the purpose of this chapter to introduce the subject of stage perspective, which concerns the dancer's relation to his audience. Space is limited, but if the reader, at the end of the chapter, feels that he has grasped its meaning, he will be in a position to work out the details for himself.

When we go to a play, we may find that an inexperienced actor is continually inaudible, because he turns his back to the audience without realising that when he does so, he should raise his voice. On this occasion, it is quite easy for the spectator to perceive what is wrong with the actor's performance. In the case of a performance of ballet, exactly the same critical principles may be applied—except that instead of audibility, degrees of visibility become the most important consideration ; and any faults of this nature are far more difficult to diagnose. The additional complications of music, libretto, *décor* and choreographic design all tend to obscure individual shortcomings, which may be ruining the production. Indeed, lack of stage perspective causes a bad performance more often than lack of technical skill.

Stage perspective may conveniently be divided into two categories : (i) *physical perspective*, or the view of himself which the *soliste* consciously displays to his audience ; (ii) *stage perspective*, or the view displayed by the dancers who are taking part in some general choreographic scheme.

There are certain rules governing the view of himself which a dancer displays to his *maître de ballet*. However, these do not prepare the dancer adequately for theatrical performance, unless the teacher insists that his pupil is perpetually conscious of an imaginary auditorium throughout his entire training. Although

CROISÉE   À LA QUATRIÈME   ÉCARTÉE   EFFACÉE
DEVANT   DEVANT

ABOVE: THE EIGHT DIRECTIONS OF THE BODY.

nothing can replace actual experience of stage and auditorium, yet an exacting teacher who can give demonstrations and criticisms, can do much to prepare his pupil for his professional *début*. For in this way, the intensely difficult art of *self-visualisation* becomes second nature to the dancer.

"The ballet was performed—
.....but not always to
ourselves"

At the base of these two pages are sketches of the *eight directions of the body*. They are often performed as a Cecchetti exercise, and are a study in perspective, as well as in *adage*. The importance of the *directions of the body*, as a study in balance, weight-adjustment, nobility and grace of carriage, is usually appreciated by the dancer and his teacher; care is often taken to present the correct angle of each pose, but the main object of this exercise tends to become overlooked, in that the dancer of to-day often fails to apply the precepts of the *eight directions* to all other movements in dancing.

Herein lies one of the principal reasons which cause a dancer who gives a brilliant technical performance in class, to disappoint us on the stage ; conversely, here lies the reason whereby the dancer who has only moderate technical capabilities, but a highly-developed instinct for self-visualisation, can employ this sense on the stage to bewitch us into believing he has performed technical feats far out of his reach. (How often have you heard a dancer's success hailed with the comment—" But he can't do a *thing* in class ! ")

Very few people are born already equipped with an instinctive feeling for stage perspective, and very few teachers and dancers concern themselves with the subject which is closely akin to good showmanship, and therefore probably considered slightly vulgar. Nevertheless, the perpetual back-views and distortions accorded by the dancer of to-day to his audience are as unprofessional as they are contrary to the traditions of stage etiquette.

À LA SECONDE   ÉPAULÉE   À LA QUATRIÈME DERRIÈRE   CROISÉE DERRIÈRE

LINES AT BASE OF SKETCHES INDICATE ANGLE FROM WHICH POSITIONS SHOULD BE VIEWED.

2. *PRACTICAL PERSPECTIVE*

One of the greatest difficulties to be solved in the training of a ballet-student is to find a method by which he can be taught to understand the adaptation of classroom technique to that of a stage performance. In the classroom, he faces his teacher, who usually tells him that similarly, on the stage, he must " keep his face to the audience ". This injunction generally constitutes the student's entire training in stagecraft.

Clearly, this is quite inadequate, and at the foot of the page is the Cecchetti solution to the problem. The square in the upper part of the sketch is a diagram of the " Cecchetti stage " ; the lower sketch shows the same stage, put to fanciful use. The classroom floor is treated in just the same way ; the pupils memorise the direction numbers, 1-8. If the teacher says " Stand facing 5, turn your head to 2 ", the pupil stands facing the teacher, and turns his head to his left. The centre of the classroom and the centre of the stage are always borne in mind, for the *soliste* who makes a bad guess at the exact middle of the stage will spoil his *variation*, cause his poses to seem off-balance and give the audience the impression that they are only seeing half a performance.

N.B.—The *eight directions of the body*, the terms *effacée* and

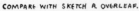

1.

2.

COMPARE WITH SKETCH A. OVERLEAF.   COMPARE WITH SKETCH D. OVERLEAF.

croisée, the *open* and *closed positions of the feet*, etc., are technical designations which always remain the same, whichever way the dancer is facing. If you were in the position *croisée devant*, for example (see sketch on p. 36) and the stage revolved with you on it, you would be *croisée devant* the whole way round.

The sketches 1-4, above and below, relate to the drawings of a detail from the *mazurka* in LES SYLPHIDES, shown on the two succeeding pages. Fig. 1 shows the conclusion of a *grand jeté en tournant* as we often see it to-day. This view of a dancer, at such a moment, is by no means confined to performances of LES SYLPHIDES alone, but as this ballet fails completely when each moment is not carefully studied, it is easily understood that lack of stage perspective is sure to cause an unsuccessful performance. Fig. 2 could have a place as a pose in a ballet—but not when it indicates failure to " get round " after the *grand jeté*, at the same time spoiling the beautiful pose which succeeds it (sketch E overleaf). The diagrams 3 and 4 show the visual difference between the incorrect position, 1, above, and the correct position, A, overleaf.

3.   4.

3. A DETAIL FROM THE MAZURKA IN "LES SYLPHIDES"

The sketches on these pages show an excerpt from the *mazurka* in LES SYLPHIDES, beginning with the conclusion of a *grand jeté en tournant*. This movement directly succeeds the sequence shown on pp. 56-57, in the chapter on "Music and the Dancer". The demonstrator is the same.

E

↑ LINE OF STAGE

LES SYLPHIDES is a ballet of incomparable beauty, but it cannot be performed with success unless the dancers possess unusual interpretative powers. Present-day performances—one cannot say "interpretations"—leave the newcomer in pardonable doubt as to the cause of the widespread enthusiasm occasioned by the original production; ballet-veterans quite simply never want to see it again. A great deal of criticism has been levelled at the dancers, on the score of insufficient poetic feeling, etc.; but when we remind ourselves that even a poet cannot function unless he has a certain mastery over his own language, we realise that a dancer cannot give a poetic interpretation of a rôle when she has not been trained either musically or with regard to the elements of stage perspective.

The delicacy of the poses A and D would be lost if addressed to the backcloth. If the pose on sketch 2 on the preceding page be substituted for D, then sketch E, on the right, becomes a sorry spin-cum-scramble, instead of the lovely *attitude* shown here. (Compare with direction *croisée derrière* on p. 39.)

The small sketches, B and C, show the transitional steps, so that anyone who wishes to scrutinise or essay this particular sequence may do so. It would be well to note that the demonstrator was able to give a detailed account, not only of each pose, but of each intermediary movement in slow motion, also to provide an excellent practical reason for each one.

N.B.—The sketches on these pages, and throughout the book, are not intended to represent inflexible rules, but are to be taken as examples from which the reader can form judgements, rules and substitutions of his own. (For further observations on *Perspective*, see Chapter VII, " On Partnering.")

44

(7. 8 & 9: pas de bourrée)

4. TOUR EN RENVERSÉ EN
DEHORS. (Two versions.)

Here are two versions of ren-
versés en dehors, the one above

of the head. When the reader bears in mind that these turns must be performed in about 2-3 seconds, that the value of either will be lost if any of the movements are "faked" or *performed at the wrong angle to the spectator*, he will understand that a knowledge of perspective must be second nature to the dancer. There is no time for reflection.

CHAPTER V

ON " LINE "

1. *EXPLANATION*

The first purpose of this chapter is to disabuse the reader of the idea that a " good *line* " and a " good *arabesque* " signify one and the same thing. First let us examine briefly the reasons which have given rise to this confusion.

The primary cause is associative. An *arabesque* is a pose which is easily recognised, and one with which the ballet-lover and the student of ballet first become familiar. Consequently the student, hearing constantly linked references to *line* and *arabesque*, draws the inevitable inference, viz., that a dancer who has a " beautiful line " must have a " high *arabesque* ", (see fig. 8) and this mis-conception has now been communicated to the lover of ballet as well.

In reality, a sense of *line* is not achieved by acrobatic means, but is a feeling for physical harmony which should form a never-absent part of the dancer's sensibility, and which he should be able to adjust to every aspect of dancing, whether academic, romantic, dramatic, rhythmic or characteristic. Even a dancer who has an unpleasing *arabesque* (perhaps for physical reasons) may quite possibly possess good *line* in movement, which the possessor of a " high *arabesque* " would do well to study.

As *line* relates to every posture in dancing, so it relates to all movements in dancing. A dancer who has studied the *line* of each pose, but who has failed to apply the same principles to the movements which link the poses together, is not a dancer at all.

Although the two terms are not synonymous, it is obvious that the principles which govern the use of *line* should also be applied to *arabesques*. A brief portrayal of the generally accepted rules appear at the head of the opposite page.

The word *arabesque* is derived from a form of Moorish ornament, in which the use of curves, and of the diagonal line, will be noticed (fig. 1). Musically, the term conveys a form of melodic ornamenta-tion of a somewhat voluptuous nature. Hence, geometrically speaking, the formation of a right angle, which is produced by raising the leg in a line with the hip whilst keeping the body up-right, has little apparent relation to the implication of the word *arabesque*, which suggests a certain flowing quality and which the " pin-man " (fig. 2) does not possess, in spite of the fact that *his pose is technically correct*. This pose should be practised by the dancer who is interested in controlling his body, so that his *line*

1.   **2.**   **3.**   **4.**   **5.**   **6.**

can be modified according to his personal taste and not restricted by physical limitations.

According to the opinion most general amongst teachers of taste, the *line* of an *arabesque* should run unbroken from the fingers of the highest arm, through the body, to the toe of the extended leg. (See figs. 3-6.) Although the back must be supported and made as straight as possible, a slight curve in the body is dictated by Nature, and therefore makes the *line* at once more pliable and graceful.

The supporting leg, whether straight or bent, serves as a sort of pivot, like the centre of a pair of scales and, whatever angles are employed, the *line* itself should remain the same.

The sketches on this page show: fig. 1, part of a Moorish arabesque; 2, the theoretical position for a *first arabesque*; 3-6, a simplified version of the use of *line* in various *arabesques*, the course of which is emphasised by dots; fig. 7, a spineless caricature of fig. 2, this familiar example of an *arabesque* shows that the entire purpose of the pose has been overlooked; fig. 8, another familiar distortion of an arabesque, which is usually described as " doing the splits on one leg ".

7.

TURN SKETCH ROUND THIS WAY FOR VIEW OF THE "SPLITS"

A "HIGH ARABESQUE."

8.

2. *INTERPRETATION*

" *The movements of the soul . . . cannot be limited to a fixed number of gestures.*" Thus Noverre addresses all those who would try to make a rule-of-thumb for all postures in dancing ; heaven knows in what contempt he would have held that school of thought which would limit *line* in dancing solely to the execution of *arabesques* ! The drawing below shows Mlle Spessivtzewa as Giselle. The line is apparently simple—so nearly straight from brow to toe, but in the course of that line, the whole feeling of this romantic ballet is so subtly conveyed, that we may be taken in by the gentle relaxation of this superlative artist. Anything further removed from a " high *arabesque* " would be hard to find ; it is an excellent example of *interpretative dancing*, in which *line* allied to feeling plays an indispensable part, and without which ballets such as the second act of GISELLE, and LES SYLPHIDES virtually cease to exist.

Olga Spessivtzewa. "Giselle."

(*from a contemporary photograph.*)

Anna Pavlova: "The Dragonfly"
(from a contemporary photograph)

This drawing of Mlle Pavlova as the Dragonfly is another out-standing example of the combination of *line* and feeling. This pose is as vivacious and skilful as the other is nostalgic and re-strained. *Below :* Sketch A shows an insensitive pose with no *line* at all; the position resembles a propped-up picture-frame (B), whereas Spessivtzewa's interpretation can best be compared with the work of Nature (c). D shows a muddled version of Pav-lova's pose, purposeless, and with that familiar view of under-neath the chin, it resembles a shapeless parcel (E). F shows a floral equivalent for Pavlova's pose.

4

50

3. *MISINTERPRETATION: AN UGLY DUCKLING?*

" A dancer who has studied the *line* of each pose, but who has failed to apply the same principles to the movements which link the poses together, is not a dancer at all "—and certainly she doesn't deserve the title of ballerina.

The girl is practising her *adage* from SWAN LAKE with two friends. Fig. 1, a well-placed *arabesque* supported by the Prince ; 2, she leaves the Prince ; so far, so good. She is going to do a *posé*, and fig. 3 shows her as she decides where she will put her foot. In fig. 4 she has forgotten she is a princess, or a ballerina, or half a swan. With an unnecessarily high *développé*, hunched shoulders and posterior to match, she makes an ungainly prelude to the appealing *arabesque* which follows (fig. 5). In this case, it is doubtful whether she could hold this low *arabesque* without the aid of the Prince's friend ; after her enormous *développé*, unaided she would probably land flat on her face.

She leaves the Prince's friend, and this time it is her dread that the Prince's hand will be out of reach for her coming *arabesque penché*. With crab-like movements, she pivots on her heels (figs. 6-7), whilst expressions ranging from acute anxiety to heartfelt relief succeed one another on her face. Fig 8, with the *arabesque penché* she turns into a princess again, but only temporarily ; for fig. 9 shows a moment which should never occur :—the Prince and the Princess, face to face, on bent knees, *en route* for their next pose.

CHAPTER VI

ON MUSIC AND THE DANCER

1. *DEFINITION*

The question of the musicality of a dancer is often the subject for discussion, but a definition of the matter is seldom attempted. Consequently, many of the discussions are conducted at cross-purposes. In the following pages the subject is introduced briefly, in its relation to present-day ballet. There is not sufficient space to discuss all objections and exceptions, and the reader must supply these controversial pros and cons himself.

In the eighteenth century, in his *Letters* on dancing, Noverre directs some well-aimed missiles at the unmusical dancer of his day. We can scarcely do better than to quote one passage here :

" *There are ears which remain out of time with, and insensible to, the most striking music ; there are a lesser number of them which feel the time, but cannot seize upon its niceties ; lastly, there are others which appreciate naturally and easily the most difficult melodies. Mlle Camargo and M. Lany enjoyed that precious gift and that precision which accord to dancing a spirit of vivacity and gaiety which is never found in those dancers who have less sensitiveness and delicacy of hearing . . . a dancer can have very delicate feeling and not reveal it to the spectator, if he do not possess the art of using with ease the tendons by which the instep is used.*"

One of the most interesting points contained in the above extract, is in the nature of the reference to Camargo. It is generally known that she was a great dancer, but her artistic gifts have become somewhat obscured by her fame as the historical *danseuse* who shortened her skirts, and scandalised the contemporary Grundies with a glimpse of twinkling ankles. Noverre, however, singles her out for her remarkable musicality.

A sixteenth-century poet named Marino, in his poem " Adonis " described the dance of Terpsichore, in the course of which he alludes to the execution of *pirouettes*, beats, *entrechats*, *arabesques*, etc., in the most exact manner, by describing the movements themselves and without, of course, using our technical terminology ; in addition, at the outset of the stanza :

" *Her attention is fixed, on the harmonious sounds, while she arranges her steps in preclude. . . . Marking each note, minding every pause, promptly she obeys each phrase of the music, which she respects as mistress of every motion.*"

A dancer famed for his musicality was Carlo Blasis. In his book, *The Code of Terpsichore* (1830), he describes how he used to induce his father to extemporise on the pianoforte, whilst he (Carlo) " *endeavoured to follow his musical intentions* ". He was given this idea by the celebrated dancer, M. Gardel, who said that the equally famous M. Dupré used thus to "*accustom his ear to catch measures and rhythms*" with greater rapidity.

From these extracts and quotations it will be seen that dancers, and in particular choreographers, in every century have been deeply concerned with the relation of music to dancing. In its primitive form, the question of musical relationship was that of making most of the music oneself, by the means of clapping, stamping and singing. Now that the study of bodily movement has been allowed to become separated from the study of music, the question of the relationship between movement and music has grown increasingly underestimated and misunderstood.

Imagine a band of primitives conducting a burial ceremony with songs and dances. They do not need to be told that their expressions must range from solemnity to anguish, that their gestures must be chastened and slow, and that they must keep time to the rhythms of their songs ; for each one knows the music and its meaning backwards, and he is also well acquainted with the melancholy character of the ceremony. Compare this example to the various musical-dramatic moments in the stage invention, GISELLE, and examine the faces and gestures of the gathering on these occasions. The great gulf formed by civilisation, which divides these two examples of music and movement, should be bridged by art, and trodden by Terpsichore.

In the normal ballet classroom, the student's musical training

Marie CAMARGO 1710-1770
(from the painting by Nicolas Lancret)

consists of being told to " keep time to the music ". That is to say, he is taught to understand that music is divided into bars, some of which contain two beats, others three, four or six beats, and so on ; if he can always remain " on the beat ", he is considered musical ; if he can still recognise the beat, even during the usual orchestral fluctuations of timing, he is accounted very musical indeed.

The trouble starts when we realise that music contains more than bars and beats. Even if a dancer can hold his pose for exactly the same duration as one of the instrumentalists holds his note, it does not follow that therefore the dancer is musical. Music is made up of phrases, and tone, as well as of time, and together these elements give music that power to move us to corresponding emotions ourselves. This is the very substance of music, and may be termed the *emotional content*.

If a dancer is trained without continual reference to this emotional content, the result is that he develops a " deaf ear " for tone and phrasing ; he disregards the obvious melodic message and the feeling of the music in order to decipher and to display to the spectator his ability to recognise the number of beats in a bar under any circumstances.

It is well known that many people who have not the least technical knowledge of music, nor any melodic or rhythmic sense themselves, can yet be profoundly moved by the various musical colours and moods. Hearing emotional music, and confronted by a dancer who is apparently unaffected by that emotion, such a person will probably condemn the dancer as a " cold " performer. What he means is that the dancer is not in accompaniment with the music. Any number of brilliant steps, matchless technique, the correct number of beats in a bar—all are of no avail. The dancer may be performing at the same time as, and in time with, the music, but he is not interpreting it if he is emotionally unresponsive.

It has been affirmed that it is sufficient to teach a dancer to " keep time " during his student days, and that musical interpretation, as already described, is in the province of the choreographer. Undeniably, it is the first consideration of the choreographer to see that his ballets, and all who take part in them, are one with the music. To present him with a group of performers who know something of " time " and nothing whatever of tone and phrasing, is to ask him, musically speaking, to educate his own dancers, in the short space of time allowed for the rehearsal of a ballet. This he will try to do, but what a waste of his time, and how disheartening, to struggle to describe feelings, impulses and shades of atmosphere which cannot be put into words, but only shown in movement, by a capable exponent !

The choreographer is an artist, i.e. one of those people who get ideas from the thin air, and he relies on dancers to bring those ideas to life. Therefore it is easily understood that the consummation of his ideas must be limited by the dancer's own limitations.

It is said that those who are born already able to swim, find it difficult to teach others to do so. For the same reason, those who have been born with a highly developed musical sensitivity find it difficult to appreciate the problems of those who are not similarly gifted. This musical dilemma would be greatly reduced if exercises could be arranged which feature the interpretation of different pieces of music which are of the same *time*, but of *various moods and emotional content*. In this way dancers would learn to respond to this intangible but powerful element in music, and choreographers would gain greater inspiration from watching classes, as well as increased co-operation from the dancers.

When the dancer is one with the music, it is immaterial whether he is following the music or whether the music is following him. When the harmony between the respective movements in dancing and music is complete, the result is so compelling that it will captivate even the most unmusical spectator.

In these pages I have done my best to describe the quality of musicality in words ; on the two following pages, I have attempted to clarify the matter a little further, with the help of sketches.

The sketches are based on part of Fokine's ballet, LES SYLPHIDES ; since this work is referred to so frequently in this book, here is a sketch of Marie Taglioni as La Sylphide, in which rôle she first introduced the romantic *tutu*, as adapted for LES SYLPHIDES.

Marie Taglioni as
"La Sylphide", 1832.

(from a contemporary lithograph)

A.

EDGE OF STAGE

B.

C.

X
(A. AGAIN)

X
(A. AGAIN)

Meno mosso

A — B .... A — C .... A — D .... E .... *f (grand jeté en tournant ......*

p sostenuto

KEY TO SKETCHES:

2. Demonstration

"LES SYLPHIDES"—A DETAIL FROM THE MAZURKA

The sketches on these pages show an example of the musical interpretation of the accompanying bars of music. The usual demonstration consists, approximately, of three repetitions of sketches A and C, which shows a disregard for the instructions p and f; i.e. *pianissimo*, inscribed under bar A—C, which grows to *fortissimo* (bar E).

Sketch E is the preparation for the *grand jeté en tournant*, which figures in the chapter on "Stage Perspective" (pp. 42-43).

The interpretation selected, and shown here, is that of Celia Franca. Natur-

D.

E.

ally musical, she has also made a serious study of music; which means that whilst a musical interpretation is second nature to her, she is fully conscious of all she does.

A dancer who has had a musical training *as part of ballet training* is sufficiently rare to be remarkable.

For further reference to musicality in relation to several dancers, see Chapter VII, p. 63, "On Partnering", where "teamwork" is briefly discussed.

3. *THE RHYTHMICAL DANCER*

In the first part of this chapter, we have examined briefly the meaning of the term *musical* when used in conjunction with the ballet-dancer. We have seen that the genuinely musical dancer has interpretative powers which can reveal to us all facets and qualities of the music, whether they be lyrical or *staccato*, emotional or academic, with complete accuracy and timing.

Under the heading of musicality, a small group of dancers stands out with startling clarity ; the members of this group are the *rhythmical dancers*. As this chapter would be incomplete unless some tribute were paid to them, here it is, in the form of an analysis.

We can begin by affirming that the rhythmical dancer senses musical *tempe* with such ease that he can afford to " play with the time " ; in the words of Mr. Percy Scholes, in his notes on *good rhythm in performance*, " such slight but purposeful departures from regularity suggest life as opposed to mechanism ".

It is these " departures from regularity "—slight anticipations of the beat, infinitesimal lingerings after it—which provide us with that feeling of excitement and satisfaction. We sense that the dancer is using every part of his body to make the musical rhythm spring to visible life, that he has exchanged his very heart-beats for the pulsation of the music ; we have complete confidence that the dancer will only " quarrel " with the time of the music for some purpose of his own. He is incapable of offending our sense of time, but never tires of pretending he is about to do so ; hence the excitement.

It would be natural to assume that the superlatively rhythmical dancer cannot use his especial gifts choreographically, as it is obviously impossible to teach a company of dancers to execute steps in this highly personal manner, thus one might logically suppose that the rhythmical dancer must remain an inspiring *soliste*. Fortunately, this is not so ; choreography is not a matter of the multiplication of scores of small ideas, but rather the art of suggesting details by the means of a general scheme. Thus the rhythmical dancer can codify certain elements in his own performance, which can be taught to most dancers, and can become in this way a highly personal form of choreography.

Of all those who have succeeded in work of this *genre*, the ballets of Léonide Massine, and of Walter Gore (once his pupil), are the most remarkable. The work of Jerome Robbins, a new choreographer, whets the appetite by displaying the same mastery of rhythm.

Noverre, writing on music, remarks on the acute sense of rhythm and timing displayed by the people of whole provinces in

Germany. "This natural and innate taste for music brings in its train a similar liking for dancing. . . . Counterpoint, which is undoubtedly the touchstone of the most delicate ear, presents the least difficulty to them. . . . " One wonders what would have happened to that countryside gusto for rhythm, if it were subjected to the average ballet-dancer's training of to-day. Would it survive ?

Nowadays the most remarkable exponents of an innate sense of rhythm of an astonishing quality are the negroes, whom we see all too seldom on the stage. Singular rhythmical dancing is still practised by Spanish villagers, but Argentina, who showed its very soul all over the world, dances no more. Perhaps the highest standard of natural rhythm, as described on this page, is to be seen in the largest *palais de danse* in the big towns, where love of rhythm is still the reason which causes the strangest mixture of people to go there and dance. And perhaps—who knows ?— visits to these dancing-palaces would keep alive in ballet-dancers that vivacious, careless and prompt reaction to basic musical rhythms, of which their present-day training tends to deprive them.

Léonide Massine in LE TRICORNE

Walter Gore in MR. PUNCH

CHAPTER VII   ON PARTNERING

1. PAS DE DEUX FROM "*LES SYLPHIDES*"

Extract from "*Grande Valse Brillante*" by Chopin:
a *pas de deux* from "*Les Sylphides*."

④

⑤

PARTNERING & PERSPECTIVE:
for explanation
see overleaf.

1st lift →

⑥

⑩

⑪

2nd lift →

⑫

for ⑭ and ⑮
repeat sketches
② and ③

⑯

⑰

3rd lift

X   X

2. *PRELIMINARY NOTE ON PERSPECTIVE IN PART-NERING* (*illustrated on previous page*)

The sketches which relate to the chapter on " Perspective " (p. 38) are nos. 5, 11 and 17 ; as these are three lifts which show a certain use of perspective in choreography.

On p. 41, fig. 1, the dancer who presents a confused and negative view of herself to the spectator, with her leg pointing directly at him, has been used to show a faulty stage sense. Here, in nos. 5 and 11, the girl is in a somewhat similar posture, with her leg pointed at the audience, her face hidden by her arm, and most of her torso—and her partner—hidden by quantities of billowing tarlatan. In this case, the two lifts, 5 and 11, are part of a choreographic scheme designed to build up the *pas de deux* to an effective finale, which is achieved as shown by sketch 17, where the same lift is performed for the third time,—but on this occasion the dancer travels sideways, thus displaying the most beautiful view of the lift to the audience.

3. *PRACTICAL OBSERVATIONS*

The three lifts by themselves are sufficient to illustrate the point described above. The series of sketches has been completed, however, including the main transitional movements, in order to illustrate some notes on partnering.

From a careful study of the sketches, it will be seen that the girl and the man are *dancing together*. That is to say, in the time which it takes to perform this extract (say approximately 15 seconds) there are a number of occasions when the pair might bang their heads together, miss a lift by being too far apart, trip each other, and many more occasions when they might simply look ungainly. For instance, take nos. 10, 11 and 12, which show an awkward forward lift, face to face ; unless there is complete co-operation here, the two dancers will find themselves in a most unbecoming and precarious posture, beginning and ending with a general scramble.

Perhaps it is worth adding that in each of the lifts the man has to walk a few steps with the girl lifted. If she tries to travel herself, instead of leaping straight upwards and leaving her partner to propel her through the air, she will either throw the man completely off his balance ; or else she will find herself leaping alone, whilst the man runs after her, vainly trying to catch her waist.

Further awkward moments will occur throughout any *pas de deux*, if the man rises on his toes when he lifts his partner. She will feel utterly insecure, as the man on his points will certainly rock unsteadily backwards and forwards.

To be a good partner, whether male or female, is by no means a matter of technique alone.   In the first act of the ballet, GISELLE, the encounters of the village maiden with her disguised lover, Count Albrecht, must range from the gay nonsense of a rustic courtship to the tragedy of Giselle's madness and death ; neither the ballerina nor her partner can evoke the emotional atmosphere unaided, and between them they must make the old story live, and convince themselves and their audience that the laughter and tragedy are taking place for the first time. Albrecht's horror and remorse at the death of Giselle must prepare the audience for the nostalgic scene which follows, in which the ghost of Giselle floats compassionately amongst the damp trees and tries to save her lover from the doom which awaits him. Those contemporary photographs which show Karsavina and Nijinsky as Giselle and Albrecht repay repeated study, for they retain an atmosphere of artistic unity which should inspire every modern dancer.   (See sketch on p. 65.)

In 1830, a *balletomane*, impressed with a *pas de deux* performed by Marie Taglioni and Jules Perrot, pays them this tribute :
" *Each responded to the other.   They moved together as though swayed by the same breath of wind ; they sank and rose as if moved by a common impulse . . . together they plunged into pale mists ; they rose, one with her ineffable voluptuousness, the other with his temerity and audacity, both in the most melodious harmony.*"

With regard to the team-work of a whole company, here, every consideration applicable to the individual dancer must be subordinated to consideration of the performance as a whole. (In support of this statement, the reader has only to consider what would happen on a battlefield if each member of an army insisted on carrying out his own personal plan of campaign.) For example, take the case of a *pas de quatre* in which each dancer must perform identical steps ; although each one may be equally musical, the general appearance of the four will be far from tidy unless they co-operate with one another ; the angles of the limbs, the height of the leaps, must be agreed upon, and regularly practised and adhered to.   How many *ensembles* have been spoiled because one dancer jumps just a little higher than the others, and lands constantly out of time with his companions ? Such a dancer must learn cheerfully to conserve his superior elevation for his solos.

The spirit of selfless co-operation can make a group of dancers into a powerful company.

CHAPTER VIII

ON CLASSIFICATION

1. *ON THE CLASSIFICATION OF BALLETS*

This chapter is mainly concerned with the use of the two adjectives, *classical* and *romantic*, as these two designations are most familiar to the ballet-goer, and most often misused. Definitions of the various types of modern ballets can only be attempted in this book to illustrate certain other points ; their present classification must be left to the ballet-magazine editor, and their ultimate value to the theatre-going public.

The argument for our discussion is as follows : Although the classical *tutu* is easily distinguishable from the romantic *tutu* (see p. 68), this costume cannot be regarded with safety as the sole indicator of the nature of the ballet in which it is employed ; moreover, although the terms " classical " and " romantic " have a certain meaning when linked with the word *tutu*, when used in a more general sense their significance is far less clearly defined. To take a simple example, although LES SYLPHIDES is perhaps the most well-known of all *romantic* ballets, yet it can also be described as *classical*, in the sense that it has earned its place amongst standard works of art, and has become a classic.

A development of this situation is, that when someone refers to a ballet as " one of the classics " it is often left open to doubt whether the ballet in question has a place in tradition, such as PETROUCHKA, or whether the allusion refers to the academic form of ballet technique such as that employed in SWAN LAKE.

The expression " classical ballet " has now come to have a meaning of its own, but when used loosely it leads to confusion and cross-purposes. For example, a " classical *pas de deux* " now means an excerpt from, let us say, AURORA'S WEDDING, but a *pas de deux*, arranged with the exclusive use of the academic ballet technique, may also be described as " a classical *pas de deux* ".

Therefore, to avoid further complications, it would be advisable to substitute the word " academic " for " classical " on all suitable occasions.

Academic ballet conveys the traditional development of pure technique. The complete mastery of it should enable the dancer to perform any feat demanded by any choreographer, modern or otherwise. Although every movement in the academic technique is rigidly controlled, its aim is not to limit the dancer but to reward him with a physical and artistic freedom unheard of in other schools of movement.

Three famous ballets from the classical repertoire featuring the use of the academic technique are SWAN LAKE, THE SLEEPING PRINCESS, and COPPÉLIA. Examples of famous romantic ballets are GISELLE, LES SYLPHIDES and CARNAVAL.

2. *ON THE CLASSIFICATION OF THE BALLERINA*

In order to compare the different characteristics of ballerinas, perhaps the most reasonable method is to begin by studying two of the great traditional rôles, and the various gifts and qualities which they demand of their performers.

The ballerina's solos in SWAN LAKE are composed of pure academic technique and designed to display to the fullest degree the technical and authoritative capabilities of the Swan Princess

Famous Partners:
Tamara KARSAVINA &
Vaslav NIJINSKY
in "Giselle" (1910)
From a contemporary
photograph.

and not to evoke any particular mood or atmosphere ; the latter is left to the designer of *décor* and costumes. This means that if the ballerina cannot introduce any emotional content into her rôle, but can give a performance which is technically perfect, the sparkle of her faultless execution will be sufficient in itself, as it has a fire and an appeal of its own.

In the solos of Giselle, the academic technique is employed once more, and is by no means easy to execute, but here it is used as a means to a romantic end. A Giselle who has only technique, and no emotional capability, is a theatrical and artistic atrocity.

Therefore, it will be seen that a successful Swan Princess is by no means whatsoever a potentially successful Giselle.

3. *ON THE CLASSIFICATION OF THE DANSEUR*

In Chapter I we have seen that, physically speaking, there are two main types of dancer, viz. (i) the *jarreté*, most suited to lyrical and academic rôles ; (ii) the *arqué*, who is brilliant and rhythmical. Very exceptional is the dancer who conforms to neither of these two categories. But it cannot be stressed too clearly that either type, if he is suitably intelligent, accomplished and adjustable, should be able to give an interesting performance of the rôles which are physically suited to his opposite.

Those dancers of the *jarreté* type, to whom are usually assigned the rôles of the *danseurs nobles*, should be able to give a different but stimulating interpretation of the more robust type of rôle usually entrusted to the *arqué* dancer, bringing to bear on his movements all his innate grace and fluidity, and intelligence and vivacity to his deportment.

The *arqué* dancer, when it is demanded that he should assume the rôle of *danseur noble*, usually surprises the spectator at the outset by his *attaque* and virility ; secondly, his supreme control of his muscles and movements lends him an especial dignity, which quite atones for that more languid grace associated with the *jarreté* dancer.

4. *ON GENERAL CLASSIFICATION*

The desire to classify human beings is an excellent thing, in the right degree. To have a knowledge of ballet, and to enjoy a certain discrimination, one must be able to recognise the different types of performer. However, such classification can become a peril and directly opposed to any artistic advancement, if wielded like a whip over a company of dancers.

Under the latter circumstances, a girl may find herself confined to a pigeon-hole labelled *Classical and Technical Rôles Only*. In

THE ILLUSION OF CLASSICAL-ROMANTIC BALLET

"*'Tis impossible to describe that with the hand, which never entered into the imagination*" (G. P. Bellori, 1664). Sketches A: Prince Siegfried watches his lady turn into a swan, and fly away. Scene B: The picture Siegfried must evoke, and convey to the audience. Scene C: If Siegfried does not really follow with his eyes the flight of the swan, then this is the picture he will convey to his audience.

certain cases, it is obviously right that she should remain there (every aspiring Pavlova cannot be allowed to inflict on the public her version of the Dying Swan.) Nevertheless, if the girl is intelligent, as well as a successful classical dancer, the odds are that she could acquit herself well in a dramatic rôle, and benefit from the experience. If, in spite of this latent ability, she is kept rigidly in her pigeon-hole " Classical Dancer Only ", her best work will soon begin to flag, and she will be an example of *art held tongue-tied by authority*, which is a sign of mediocrity in the direction of the company.

In conclusion, it may be affirmed that there are as many types of dancer as there are great dancers. Two human beings are seldom exactly alike in every respect, physically and morally, and we can only use similes with safety when describing the separate qualities of a dancer.

Thus, we can say that a young man has the rhythm of a Massine, that he is as light as a Nijinsky, and that he resembles such-and-such a dancer in physique. But if this young man has the makings of a great dancer, we shall—and ought to—find ourselves at a loss to say exactly what " type " he is. He is his own type, although he may model himself on a score of others. His magic is the magic of art : built on tradition, but ever original.

One genius can only be said to resemble another, in that the other is a genius also.

Contemporary classical tutu. Galina Ulanova in Swan Lake (from a photograph)

Contemporary Romantic tutu: costume for a Wilis in Giselle by Hugh Stevenson.

CHAPTER IX

ON STYLE AND CHARACTER

1. *ON STYLE*

Up to the present, we have attempted certain analyses and definitions in these pages, and have discussed various components of ballet with the purpose of discovering how the dancer can rid himself of those limitations and misunderstandings which hamper his artistic and physical development, and prevent him from enjoying that absolute freedom which is the artist's right. Now we come to the discussion of freedom itself.

When a student of any one of the arts has gained complete mastery over his medium, it is his own personality, expressed through his work, which will determine whether he is a true artist or not. If he has nothing of his own to add to the art he pursues, he will remain in pursuit of the true object of art ; he may be a superb technician, but he will forgo the freedom of the artist. In other words, he will lack style.

The word *style* is seldom used in connection with dancing, in the sense just described. " Style " usually relates to a method of dressing the hair, or to the cut of a costume, whereas the word " personality " is freely employed. As the possessor of a " good personality " is usually considered to have been born thus endowed, the general inference is that a person cannot develop a stage personality, unless especially gifted by Nature. This attitude does not allow for those born with dormant talents, and if we substitute the word " style " for " personality ", it at once becomes apparent that a good presence, although it may indeed be the result of natural gifts, can only be recognised on the stage by the way in which the performer presents himself to his audience, which is through the medium of his *personal style*. This presentation is an art in itself, and can be cultivated to the highest degree.

In painting and music, we can recognise a certain style because of certain repetitions in the way that the artist or composer has handled his material. In dancing, we are often dazzled by the physical and personal perfections of the performer, and nothing lasts long enough for us to consider its construction : we cannot hum a bar out of a *pas d'allégro* in order to reflect upon the dancer's personal style. When the performance is over, we are aware of a feeling of intense stimulation, and of a warmth as if we had just met an artist who is actually at work ; so we attribute the whole experience to personality, as this social expression seems far more descriptive than the unemotional word, style.

The student of ballet, however, should give great attention to the cultivation of style, which is utterly ignored by the vast majority of dancers and teachers.

To attempt to recall the style of Taglioni or her contemporaries, cannot be undertaken lightly, nor practised without the best of good taste. Perhaps it is more a question of the study of character than of style, but this will be investigated later on.

The perpetual view of the underneaths of dancers' chins is largely due to a mistaken sense of style ; to stick one's nose in the air is to confuse the dreary superiority of the departmental-stores manager with the brilliant authority of the ballerina. When every member of the *corps de ballet* advances down the stage in this mistaken " grand manner ", as far as the citizens in the stalls are concerned, not one of the girls has a face—only a chin. (For another cause of " chin-trouble ", see pp. 20 and 33.)

A last word concerning the personal style of a dancer. Ballet-students have been heard to criticise the choreography of GISELLE, particularly the *adage* in the second act. " It may be very difficult ", runs the comment. " but it is also rather *dull*. How can you make anything out of such classroom steps ? " The answer to that question, of course, is the answer to another, viz., what is personal style ? The *adage* in question begins with a very slow *développé à la seconde*, and is quite easy to recognise ; if the reader will memorise this step, and then go and watch a great ballerina performing it as Giselle, the meaning of style should become perfectly clear. (An example of lack of style may be found on pp. 50-51.)

2. ON CHARACTER

" The Joy of a *Monarch* for the news of a Victory, must not be express'd like the Extasie of a *Harlequin* on the Receipt of a letter from his Mistress. . . ." (Dryden, 1760). Whilst collecting material for this book, I have been hunting for schools of dancing which include character classes, and I have drawn what is virtually a complete blank, except in those cases where classes are given teaching the classical mime, which is of little general use, unless one is going to play, at least, the Prince's Friend in SWAN LAKE, or the part of some soloist in THE SLEEPING PRINCESS. Here we recognise the seeds of further chin-trouble being sown. In our contemporary portrayals of royalty, the kings and queens, dukes, duchesses and courtiers, instead of displaying that effortless dignity and grace compatible with their rank, usually give the impression of an overbearing superiority, with their noses well in the air. This is to confuse snobbishness with greatness, and will destroy the conviction of any court scene.

In its finer form and under ideal conditions, the academic

THREE ADAPTATIONS OF NATIONAL DRESS
FOR BALLET

M. & Mme. Paul Taglioni: Paris, 1833.
Adaptation of Styrian Peasant Dress.
(from a contemporary painting)

Nursemaid & Coachman in "Petrouchka."
Adaptation of Russian Peasant Dress.
from the design by Alexandre Benois, 1911.

The Dandy & a Peasant
Girl in "Le Tricorne."
Adaptation of Spanish Costume
by Pablo Picasso, 1919.
(from the original design)

ballet-training can be said to cover any field likely to be demanded of the dancer ; but at the present time, performances have shown that a company cannot function satisfactorily without dancers who have had, or are given, some instruction concerning the interpretation of character rôles. However well Giselle and Albrecht dance together, the performance as a whole can be sadly impaired by surrounding groups of expressionless and unschooled courtiers in the first act, and flocks of bored, earth-bound *wilis* in the second. Photographs taken during actual performances of GISELLE are a revelation : during the mad scene, a study of the groups of courtiers will usually reveal anything from boredom, to the animation of a private conversation.

Then there is the question of the choreographer who wants to produce a ballet on (for the sake of an example) a Hungarian theme. He has first to set about training his dancers ; they will be unable to grasp any of his movements unless he gives them special coaching first. This takes time and patience, and it is not really the choreographer's job, for even if the dancers had not learned the rudiments of Hungarian dancing, yet if they had been trained to pick up the main characteristics of national dancing in general, they would be far more adaptable. As it is, we see dancers performing *czardas* and *jotas* without any enjoyment, and substituting a kind of half-hearted polka for a spirited *mazurka*, and so on.

It is probably the limitations mentioned above which have caused so many of our contemporary choreographers to fall back on the mainly dramatic ballet, where an elaborate libretto is enacted by the dancers, during the course of which, dances take place as a sort of relief from the dramatic action.

3. *STYLE IN COSTUME*

The same factors which govern style in dancing also apply to *décor* and costumes. The quality for which we all search subconsciously is *subtlety*. There was a time when a tendency towards a too meticulous realism robbed the ballet of much of its magic ; this was followed by the inevitable reaction, a harsh and heavy-handed form of symbolism which divorced the art of ballet from Nature, whence it springs. To-day, both extremes are apparent ; a performance of SCHÉHÉRAZADE in the United States was remarkable for the introduction of real elephants on the stage, and most lovers of ballet are familiar with those uncomfortable " modernistic " designs which are the despair of the costumier and dancer alike.

In case the allusion to Nature seems a little obscure, this

STYLE IN COSTUME:
two versions of "Le Spectre de la Rose"

A typical modern
version of the
same costume.

Vaslav Nijinsky as
the Spirit of the Rose:
after the design by
Léon Bakst, 1911

section is illustrated with a drawing after Léon Bakst's original
design for Vaslav Nijinsky in LE SPECTRE DE LA ROSE ; beside
it is a drawing of the generally adopted modern version of this
masterpiece. It is clear that Bakst studied Nature, and he has
so arranged his costume that the mysterious element of the rose
is stressed, rather than its feminine associations. The colours
used on Nijinsky's actual costume range from rose pink to shades
of purple, red and tawny brown. In contrast, one shade of sugar-
pink is used in the modern version ; the main garment has become a kind of bathing-dress, and the head-dress a boudoir-cap.
Whereas there is every excuse for altering the design of a costume
which does not suit the wearer, this perfunctory approximation
of a beautiful design is lamentable.

In keeping with this superficiality, the choreography has
suffered much the same sort of change. Apart from Nijinsky's
famous leap, which could be repeated by no one with the exception of Stanislas Idzikowski, the emotional romanticism which
inspired the entire conception has undergone the same modifica-
tion as the costume. Losing oneself in the fascinating study of
ballet-tradition, one is apt to overlook the laws of Nature on
which that tradition is based.

CHAPTER X

PRACTICAL NOTES

1. *ON COSTUMES AND DÉCOR*

Many of our contemporary ballet-performances can be seen to fuller advantage during rehearsal than *en spectacle* on the stage. In an earlier chapter, we have examined those individual occasions, where a dancer appears brilliant in class but monotonous on the stage ; we must take a broader view of the situation, however, when the subject concerns entire ballets, and not merely the projection-powers of separate dancers.

It is quite obvious that bad performance may ruin a ballet ; but unsuitable costumes and *décor* not only ruin the dancer's performance, but can also obscure the very structure of the choreography itself.

The two worst pitfalls for the ballet-designer are (*a*) the failure to design costumes that are suitable for *movement*, and (*b*) the faulty use of colour and design. Concerning note (*a*), many costume designers fail to appreciate that the choice of material, and its cut, must be governed by a knowledge of human movement. E.g. *Paniers*, covered by heavy material look clumsy and absurd during a *pas d'allégro* (see sketches 1 and 2 opposite), moreover they reduce the wearer to a state of utter exhaustion. With more ethereal costumes, draperies, which look so effective on the design itself, may prove a nightmare to the dancer, catching at his feet, and attaching itself to projections of scenery. In both cases, the designer, the dancer *and the dressmaker* should combine to see that the costume is effective, comfortable, practicable and physically becoming to the wearer.

Regarding note (*b*), the elementary factors governing the use of colour and design, shown in their simplest form in sketches 5, 6 and 7, are often entirely overlooked. Variations of the effect suggested by no. 7 may be used for an especial purpose, but as an unconscious tendency, it may obscure much excellent choreography and confuse the dramatic action, whilst the value of the separate dancers themselves will be lost completely on the audience.

Those who are unfamiliar with ballet practice-costumes should make an effort to see Jerome Robbins' American choreographic romp, INTERPLAY. The *décor* (by Oliver Smith) consists of large expanses of cheerful, glowing colours, against which the movements of the simply-clad dancers show clearly. A more sophisticated version of the same precept may be seen in Frederick Ashton's beautiful SYMPHONIC VARIATIONS, with *décor* by Sophie Fedorovitch.

1 The sketch for a costume.

2. The same costume — in action.

3. Sketch for a draped figure.

4. Possible effect of the draperies in action.

5

6

7

Diagrams 5 · 6 · 7 prove a forgotten rule: dark colours show against a light background & vice versa: too much ornamentation, or too many similar colours, confuse the onlooker and obscure the dancer's movements.

8

The use of strong lighting will show up the dancer. Weak lighting will usually give the same effect as 7. above

9.

"INTERPLAY" (sketched from the pit.)

TAPE TACKED ON
BACK OF RIBBON

KNOT SOMETIMES
SEWN FOR
SAFETY

C

LEFT
FOOT
FRONT

E

A

TOE OF OLD
SLIPPER - SOLE
INSERTED
IN TOE

SHOE
BREAKS
HERE

INSIDE
RIGHT →
FOOT

B

DARNING

D

PETERSHAM
(to prevent vamp
splitting)

2. ON THE COMFORT OF BALLET-SLIPPERS

In the first chapter, the problems of the bow-legged dancer's feet have been mentioned, and a remedy promised. Fig A, above, shows the tendency of this type of foot, which is a constant source of worry and muscular strain to the owner, not only because of its appearance, but because it is so difficult to remain " on point ". Fig B shows a special addition to the routine darning, which combines with the use of a pad made from the sole of an old slipper to make the shoe far more comfortable, and improves the appearance of the foot into the bargain. Fig C shows that the arrangement of toes on this type of foot is inclined to make the owner turn her ankle in an ugly and dangerous manner ; D shows the remedy, by the addition of more darning. Fig E shows the high instep of the close-legged dancer, whose shoe is inclined to break, as indicated ; the only remedy here is to take an inner sole from an old shoe and stick it firmly inside the broken one. Where the vamp of the shoe is inclined to tear, this may be avoided in advance by the insertion of a piece of petersham ribbon, as shown. This will also relieve some of the tension on the sole. Lining the satin ribbons with tape has saved many a dancer from public ignomiy, and applies to all types of foot (Fig. B). Even if ballet-shoes become easier to obtain, their price is the despair of the ballet-student, so here is a way to prolong their life ; when the blocks have become too soft, a useful expedient is to soak the interior with *straw hat dye*, leaving it overnight to dry and harden.

3. *ON TUTUS AND THEIR CONSTRUCTION*

Although the *tutu* is such an indispensable item of ballet production, it is notable how seldom one sees this costume satisfactorily carried out. Fig. A, above, shows a *tutu* in which the
wire hoop is too far from the wearer's hips ; the stiffness having
left the tarlatan underskirts, the result is depressing and untidy.
B shows the powder-puff type of *tutu*—too short and too bulky.
C shows a far more satisfactory arrangement ; the hoop is not
more than 7 inches from the wearer's hips, and is edged with
four frills. *Below* : Fig. D shows the accepted silhouette for the
contemporary classical dancer. F, a classical costume as worn
at the Paris Opéra in 1860. E represents the misuse of both the
former characteristics. The dancer's legs are neither hidden nor
revealed, her figure bowdlerised. The general proportions, and
the mixture of hair style, head-dress, cloak and fan, are an awful
warning to the would-be designer.

4. *ON MAKING-UP*

Fig. A shows a girl facing her mirror. She is going to make up for LES SYLPHIDES. It will be seen that although her face is not remarkable for strength of feature, yet it is extremely pretty; she has medium colouring. B shows the same girl, as she will appear on the stage, having used a make-up which looked very nice in her dressing-room, but which disappeared under the strong stage lights. Eyebrows, chin and eyes have vanished, leaving a mask of the type which some people hang on their walls, but which cannot register any expression whatever. The forehead appears narrow and receding, and this is caused partly by the dowdy hair-style (in fig. A, the forehead looks quite adequate), and partly by the hideous angle of the wreath. There seems to be no division between neck and chin. C shows the same girl, with a make-up which will make her look naturally beautiful on the stage, and will resemble her own appearance far more closely than B. The only real adjustment she has made to her face is to apply a flesh-tint over a little of the hair on the temples, to broaden the forehead. This is usually a far safer method than to attempt to make the face look narrower by applying shadow to the cheeks. The hair-style used in fig. C also helps to broaden the forehead by masking any undue roundness or heaviness about the lower part of the face.

Fig. D shows a type of make-up affected by those who hanker after slanting eyes, and it goes with a forbidding expression ; this is splendid for a scene in an inferno, but is hardly suitable for a sylph. E shows the effect of a modish hair-style, when affected by a sylph ; she has to turn her back before one can see her wreath. The supercilious expression is suitable for an advertisement for cosmetics, but has no relation to ballet. (The original *coiffure* for the original *sylphide* can be seen in the sketch of Taglioni on p. 55 ; the later romantic *coiffure*, Spessivtzewa on p. 48.) F, an improvement on the wig of the *danseur* in LES SYLPHIDES, and for all romantic rôles of this order ; the wearer attaches a small roll of hair, exactly the colour of his own, round the nape of his neck, as shown. This dispenses with the discomfort of a wig, and the usually unbecoming hair-line other than one's own.

A final generalisation concerning make-up : in some companies, the men are advised to wear dark lipstick, and the girls a paler shade. This is forgetting the effect of theatrical lighting, under the glare of which the girls would seem to have no mouths at all, and the men would possess the legendary ruby lips. The advice should be reversed.

5. *ON THE ARRANGEMENT OF HAIR*

The designer of costumes usually indicates the way in which he wants the hair to be arranged, on his design. Occasionally, a wig solves the dancer's problem, but more often, she is called upon to effect a complicated *coiffure* with her own hair. This may involve an interpretation of a modern design, or of a drawing made many years ago. Here, then, are some general notes for the use of those who design *coiffures*, and those who have to put them into practice.

The same considerations apply to the arrangement of hair as to the design of an entire costume. It is inadvisable to be pedantic when reproducing hair-styles of a bygone fashion, especially if it is a fashion which is comparatively recent ; in which case, an exact reproduction will impart an atmosphere of fustiness and general *démodé*. On the other hand, in the case of a period *coiffure*, an obvious intrusion of the present fashion will appear vulgar and out of place (see fig. E) : A careful adaptation should be made therefore by the designer and the dancer, which escapes these two infringements of taste, but which brings out the best features of the wearer's face.

CURTAIN